3D STORY

BY RACHNA SHARMA

3D Story

Copyright © 2021 by Rachna Sharma

No part of this publication may be reproduced, distributed, or transmitted in any form or by any means, including photocopying, recording, or other electronic or mechanical methods, without the prior written permission of the author, except in the case of brief quotations embodied in critical reviews and certain other non-commercial uses permitted by copyright law.

Marigold Publishing Inc.

ISBN
978-1-7775224-4-5 (Hardcover)
978-1-7775224-1-4 (Paperback)

*To my students,
who inspire me everyday and share their stories!*

Rohan ran far away from everyone and sat by the fence.
He buried his face between his knees.

Just a moment before, everything had seemed great. It was a warm, sunny day outside! Everyone was happy and playing with one another. Emily was playing hopscotch with Maya while Adam, Jason, and Adeel were playing soccer.

Mrs. Smith looked at Rohan. He seemed very frustrated and angry. As soon as he noticed everyone staring at him, he started crying.

Mrs. Smith walked up to him and asked, "You look very upset Rohan. What's up?" Rohan couldn't speak, he just whimpered. Mrs. Smith could barely make out what he was trying to say.

"Rohan, why don't you take a minute and get a drink?" she suggested.

After having a few sips from his water bottle, Rohan started explaining, "I hate Aidan. He is always mean to me. He makes fun of me." Mrs. Smith stood there listening to Rohan as he continued to explain how Aidan had been treating him over the past few days.

"The other day, Aidan knocked over my lunch on purpose. Everything had spilled and splattered! I didn't have anything to eat and had starved all day long," Rohan complained.

Mrs. Smith called Aidan over. Before she could say anything, she noticed that Aidan had been crying too! His eyes were red and his face was covered in tears. He could barely speak.

Mrs. Smith asked, "What's wrong, Aidan?"

"Take a deep breath Aidan and try to calm down," she reminded him.
Aidan took a deep breath and then voiced, "Rohan is mean to me every day, all day long. I don't li…"

Before he could finish his sentence, "No! You are lying to get me in trouble," Rohan screamed.
"When I fell down this morning you laughed at me," Aidan shouted back.

"Yesterday, when I came to play with you, you totally ignored me and didn't let me join the game," Rohan protested.

"We were already playing and had sorted the teams. I told you that we will play together tomorrow but you looked very angry and stormed out," said Aidan.

Rohan said, "You are mean to me."

"You are mean to me too!" Aidan grumbled.

"You have each told me your own side of the story. But did you know that there's a third side to it too?" Mrs. Smith started explaining.

"You have both been rude and mean to each other. You both see your own side, but not the other's.
This is a conflict!" she continued.

"A conflict happens when two people see the same situation in two different ways and do not agree with each other. You are feeling upset because you are only paying attention to your side of what happened. She went on explaining further.

"Some people call this a 'perspective' and some call it a 'point of view'. When Aidan fell down and you laughed, Rohan, Aidan's feelings were hurt. This is one side of the story. When you, Aidan, didn't include Rohan in your game, he felt left out. This is the second side of the story."

But just before she could finish, Rohan said, "And what you are seeing, Mrs. Smith, is the third side!".

"IT IS A 3D STORY!" chuckled Rohan.

Rohan, Aidan, and Mrs. Smith each looked at one another and smiled.

Can you guess what happened next?

About the Author

Rachna Sharma has taught for over 25 years in India, Middle East, and Canada. Her many years of work with children has enriched her literary sensitivity. She continues to share her passion for sharing the voices of young children. As an immigrant, she loves Canada's diversity and would like to add more books with cultural variation on the shelves of kids' libraries at home and school. She currently teaches and lives in Ontario.

A Note to Teachers

Learning to consider a situation from a different perspective is often a difficult task for young children. It requires them to put themselves in the other person's position and imagine what they would feel like and think in a similar situation. Often kids see their point of view, which is the root cause of most schoolyard conflicts.

Reading stories to kids that bring up such problems and understanding others' perspectives can be a great tool to develop their understanding.

This story helps children to review and reflect on a conflicting situation. Teachers can read this story in the classroom to help students navigate such situations better.

Here are a few suggestions for educators to use this book in their classroom:

Mindful Talking
Bring students' attention to the first page when Rohan yells at Aidan. Discuss how we can come across as really harsh to other people when we are upset and angry. Why is the choice of words important? What made Aidan sad? What made Rohan angry? Discuss what different strategies Rohan could have used before he became upset with Aidan.

Calming Strategies
What did the teacher suggest for calming Rohan and Aidan? What are some of the strategies that you find helpful to manage yourself in such situations? Allow students to make connections and share their reflections.

Three Dimensions of a Story
Why do you think Rohan and Aidan have a different story? Are they getting each other's point of view? What is the third dimension of the story? Do we always have another side? Do we always have three sides to a story?

www.ingramcontent.com/pod-product-compliance
Lightning Source LLC
Chambersburg PA
CBHW051121110526
44589CB00026B/2998